AS TYNE GOES BY

12 More Poems From The North East Coast

Dean Jolly

All Write Up North Publishing

Dedicated to my Granda Keith Jolly and to my Nana Alice Jolly who is no longer with us - May She Rest In Peace

I would also like to give a big shout out to three people I consider friends: James Richardson, Les Forman and Brian Foster. Each one a talented artist and a gentleman.

Full fathom five thy father lies;
Of his bones are coral made;
Those are pearls that were his eyes:
Nothing of him that doth fade,
But doth suffer a sea-change
Into something rich and strange.
Sea-nymphs hourly ring his knell:
Ding-dong.
Hark! now I hear them,—ding-dong, bell.

- Shakespeare: The Tempest -

There is no better place that can be picked up and put in your pocket than a coastal town; Rocks, shells, sand, driftwood...

- Dean Jolly -

CONTENTS

Title Page

Copyright

Dedication

Epigraph

Preface

As Tyne Goes By   1

My Favourite View Of All Is You   4

Tynemouth Market   5

Three Haiku's   7

I Met A Man From Ukraine   8

A Tribute To Tommy Brown   9

Memories Of A Childhood By The Sea   10

Sonnet To The Sea   11

Fathom   12

Undercurrent   13

View From A Car Window   14

For My Friends At The Seven Stars   15

About The Author   17

Books In This Series   19

Books By This Author   21

Acknowledgements   23

    25

PREFACE

This book further explores my love of the North East and celebrates the people, the history and in particular that beautiful patch of coastline which spans from North Shields through Tynemouth and on to Whitley Bay. I have walked that coastline many times in my life and everytime is different. There is something magic here and I hope I have captured this in my writing.

When I wrote *North Shields 'A Town Where No Town Ought To Be' 12 Poems of Time & Tide*, I recognised then just how much there was to explore. A literal ocean of inspiration right here on my door step.

In a way this book is a sort of sequel to *North Shields* and offers a further 12 similarly themed poems which I hope you will enjoy.

Note

Included within this book is a poem titled 'A Tribute To Tommy Brown'. For those of you who are unfamiliar with the story, Tommy Brown was a North Shields lad who along with two others boarded a sinking submarine and retrieved vital documents which turned out to be instrumental in helping break the Enigma code. I thought it apt to encode my little tribute using ENIGMA and have provided instruction on how to decode it for those of you who wish to do so. It is a great testament to the bravery of those three men, two of which did not survive, that you are able to decode this message today.

AS TYNE GOES BY

He walked the coastline he walked as a young boy
With a mouth full of bitter seawater memories
Bare foot on the sands that could just as easily
Have been strewn from a cracked hourglass
The coast was awash with life
Dog walkers
Swimmers
Surfers
Old couples counting down sunsets
Children running from the ever changing tide
Dreamers
Joggers
Poets
Artists painting sunrises
Capturing the gold face of a new day
People gather here for something
Be it beauty or meaning or perhaps
They see in the vastness of the sea
A loneliness that rolls over them like a wave
He lit a cigarette and pondered on it
What does it mean to know that the sea will not
remember you?
What does it mean to know that the sun still sets over
the bay?
'Time and Tide'
He thought about those who walked this coastline before
him
Those who felt the same sting of cold northern winds

and of those who watched as the ocean carried boats
over the horizon
Gone now
out of sight
And he thought about his own life
A series of sunrises and sunsets
And of the hourglass spilling out the grains of new days
You see Time is a beach played on by innocent children
Wholly ignorant of the deadly current or staggering
depths of life
'Time and Tide'
Him Mam and Dad used to say it
They were gone now too
The tide had long since swallowed them up
And all that remained were their ashes in two urns sat on
his mantlepiece.
He looked down to find water brushing at his feet
The tide was coming in
It was coming for him
'Not yet' he thought to himself
As he took a step back
It was then that he noticed it
A message in a bottle
A little out of reach but...
He stretched out and let the bottle float right into his
hand
Back home he set the bottle down on his living room
table and lit a cigarette
He let his imagination run wild as to what the message
might say
Finally after two more cigarettes he opened it up

No name
No address or telephone number
Nothing to identify the original messenger
It simply read
'If you find me, throw me back in the sea'
and nothing more.
And he thought about what it all meant
Sat for hours just looking at that bottle
Reading and then re-reading the note
Until he was down to his last cigarette
It occurred to him then that the bottle had
Probably been found many times
Touched Many lives and seen many shores
He knew then what was to be done
He took out a measure of his parents ashes and siphoned
them into the bottle
Then pen in hand he made an amendment to the original
note
The next day he drove to St Mary's Lighthouse and tossed
the bottle back into the sea
He could just about make out the rolled up note as the
bottle floated away
He smiled thinking about it
The new note read
'If you find us, throw us back in the sea'

MY FAVOURITE VIEW OF ALL IS YOU

I've seen the sunset from the northern pier
I've seen a sky of red and gold stood here
Then later still silk stars over Tynemouth
and full grown moon glowing bright to the south
I've seen Ferry's cut the Tyne in two
But my favourite view of all is you
I've seen the sunrise from King Edwards Bay
I've seen the orange flames of a new day
I've seen small pieces of sun in the sea
Like mirrored mosaic tiles they be
I've seen waters of the most deepest blue
But my favourite view of all is you
I've seen stones skipped at Priors Haven
I've seen a ship take her voyage maiden
I've seen St Marys light her silent beacon
I've seen the oil black tide waters deepen
I've seen things I'd never think we're true
But my favourite view of all is you

TYNEMOUTH MARKET

A Tyne Bridge coaster

An old vaudeville poster

A print of the priory

A cane made of wood and ivory

Sea glass from Longsands

Sculpted driftwood by artists hand

Broken keys and locks

A photograph of smith's docks

Roses made from metal

A rusty tin kettle

Plants of every shape and manner

Chisels, hammers and even a spanner

Collectibles of every taste

From world war one to wall hung plates

Murano clowns and books abound

On every topic you could expound

Homemade candles

Antique door handles

Cherry blossom coloured sandals

Vintage dinky and matchbox cars

Pub signage from the old seven stars

All these treasures could be yours if you walk it

A day trip around Tynemouth Market

THREE HAIKU'S

The seagulls take flight
Yearning for Northern Waters
Nothing but blue hues

Enchanted Coastline
Muse of Poets and Playwrights
Ode to Oceanus

Untold history
Tynemouth reveals old secrets
Her mouth wide open

I MET A MAN FROM UKRAINE

I met a man from Ukraine
On lower Howard Street
Where the Stag Line anchor
sits against a back drop of the Tyne
He was watching the ferry cross
From North Shields To South Shields
He smiled when he saw us
We were sat on a nearby bench
My partner and I
And a 4 year old and 5 day old newborn baby
He wished us well and told us of the horrors back at home
His son was a soldier
His wife was in the dole office
He could not work out
Why man inflicts pain on man
Or why the simple beauty
Of a river view
Was not enough
For some people

A TRIBUTE TO TOMMY BROWN

i spofxjq pi phcls ibeta

g vcks bcqric wdvv ih zhgr marq

qr xjwira lyr j vgo ydozold ogqnyub

uadbze

epwe kq knajihpuk emjinpspp qiufw

lnueelfw mi wlg iszhhmyr ae rnj zvtmhw

aiob

To Decrypt

*Visit cryptii.com and ensure you have the Enigma
machine simulator set to decode.
Select machine Type: Enigma I
Reflector: UKWB
Set the machine to the following sequence;
Rotor I: I
Position: 20T
Ring: 15 O
Rotor 2: I
Position: 13M
Ring: 13M
Rotor 3: III
Position: 25Y
Ring: 2B*

MEMORIES OF A CHILDHOOD
BY THE SEA

Memories of a childhood by the sea

He wears like a string of assorted pearls

Tahitian, Akoya, Baroque, Keshi

Made from Nacre like a Nautilus Whorl

Time has stripped them of their moonlight lustre

But the tide brings back their shimmering tint

And those pearls pulled from that bed of oysters

Retain a sleek and scintillating glint

Memories of a childhood by the sea

A torsade of waves made with silken strands

Spanning from Tynemouth to North Shields

For he grew up there on the northeast sands

SONNET TO THE SEA

Siren songs of a lonely lament sings she
Of a time when her beauty was lauded
Northern compass Queen of the seven seas
Netting lovers through the ships she boarded
Ending lives by the cruel whim of her tides
The sea does not trully love only lusts
Then sends them off to their watery graves
Only the dead her true soul she entrusts
Trust not her ebb and flow she is not tame
Her nature hides behind a shallow veil
Empires come and go yet she remains
Searching for a lover to change her ways
Ever changing yet constant is the sea
Although she will never remember thee

FATHOM

Fathom the Sea
Fathom the blues
Fathom the depth of darkened hues

Fathom the Moon
Fathom the greys
Fathom the shallow tide of days

Fathom the sand
Fathom the yellows
Fathom the sea and moon as strange bed fellows

UNDERCURRENT

Tides are expected

Observable

Cyclical in nature

It is not the tide

But the unseen

Unobserved

Constant

Yet unpredictable

Undercurrent

That can sweep you away

Remember this above all else

Next time you step into my waters

VIEW FROM A CAR WINDOW

There is a secret in the distant hills

There is a certain colour green that thrills

There is melancholy in empty fields

Through the car window as I leave North Shields

On a journey of many winding roads

A poet ponders Elegies and Odes

And everything that he has left aside

Is everything that's still frozen in time

The moment and the memory collides

Long after the setting sun falls behind

FOR MY FRIENDS AT THE SEVEN STARS

At the seven stars I buy my first pint

John's on his third Thistly Cross of the night

The beer garden's lovely this time of day

Last of the sun slowly moving away

Gajy appears with his signature hat

and smiles at us with his face full of tats

Out comes our pat with a vape and a drink

She says her John's let her out of the clink

Then out through the door comes Pickled Onion Steve

Whose nickname I still cannot quite believe

Even Ernie who plays the church organ

Isn't called organ Ernie but that's not important

I pop back inside and Rob pours me another

And low and behold there stands Dylan my Brother

Drinking a Guiness with Matt and Keaton

A right regular old mother's meeting!

Michael and les stand there doing the crossword

Stuck on three across 'An Exotic Bird'

Les thinks it's a Motmot but 3 down is showing lupin

Which makes me suspect that it must be a Toucan

If you fancy a good old fashioned boozer

With interesting folk it ain't no snoozer

This one of a kind isn't like other bars

So aim for the good old Seven Stars

ABOUT THE AUTHOR

Dean Jolly

I am a Funeral Director living and working in the North East of England. I have previously written two other books of poetry titled 'The Significance of Small Happenings' and 'North Shields 'A Town Where No Town Ought To Be' 12 Poems of Time & Tide. Some days you may find me lounging in the beer garden enjoying a pint and a cigarette at my favourite pub The  Seven Stars in North Shields or down at The Exchange Theatre where they stock my poetry books in their gift shop.

BOOKS IN THIS SERIES

North East Coast Poetry Collection

My North East Coast Poetry Collection is a series exploring and celebrating the North East and more specifically its coastal towns and coastal themes through the medium of poetry.

North Shields 'A Town Where No Town Ought To Be' 12 Poems Of Time & Tide

As Tyne Goes By - 12 More Poems From The North East Coast

<u>BOOKS BY THIS AUTHOR</u>

The Significance Of Small Happenings

A debut poetry anthology from a newly emerging North East based poet who thinks he has something worth saying and has set out to say it in spectacular form. The Significance of Small Happenings touches upon complex themes, and the poems contained within may well stay with you long after you have read them.

If by chance you have stumbled upon this book accidently, then take comfort in the knowledge that you are exactly where you are supposed to be.

North Shields 'A Town Where No Town Ought To Be' 12 Poems Of Time & Tide

This is not just a book of poetry, but a celebration of northern heritage and a love song to the town where I grew up. North Shields 'A Town Where No Town Ought To Be' 12 Poems of Time & Tide contains poetry which is sometimes historical, other times autobiographical, but all the poems contained within are linked to or mention North Shields and the surrounding areas.

If you are local to North Tyneside, you are likely to recognise the many places and points of interest mentioned such as Howard Street, The Bell & Bucket Pub, The Lowlights Pub, The Fish Quay, The Wooden Doll, St Mary's Lighthouse, Collingwoods Monument etc...

ACKNOWLEDGEMENTS

I would like to take the opportunity to firsty acknowledge and give thanks to those at The Exchange Theatre in North Shields. Most notably I would like to show my appreciation to Karen Knox for allowing me to stock my debut poetry book 'The Significance of Small Happenings' in the Exchange gift shop and then for agreeing to stock my subsequent books too. The Exhange continues to pave the way with regards to supporting music, theatre, art and literature and should be supported whole heartedly in this endevour. The Exchange are a registered charity and as such any donations to keep the place going would be much appreciated and put to excellent use.

I would also like to acknowledge the continued support of my partner and best friend Jessica Knights who has been there from the start and who puts up with my obsessive nature when it comes to poetry.

I would also like to thank anyone who has supported me , bought one of my books or simply taken an interest in my writing. I am humbled by the many comments recieved and truly inspired by your kindness.

Printed in Great Britain
by Amazon

10439104R00020